The Bridge:

Between Cell Block A and a Miracle is Psalm 91

By Jackie Carpenter

xulon
PRE

Contents

Dedication

This book is dedicated to my wonderful husband, Larry, who married me sixteen years ago and accepted my two sons as his very own. He has always been there for us, and it will never be forgotten. Thank you, Jesus, for sending Larry to us. And to my four grandchildren: Hannah, Anna Grace, Patience and J.J. As they navigate through their own storms in life, may they always be reminded of our family's miracle, and may they always know that this awesome God will do the same for them. God bless each one of them!

Acknowledgments

To my parents, whose faith never wavered, which enabled them to survive this "pit of torment." Thank you for always giving me encouragement, even when there wasn't encouragement to give.

I waited patiently for the Lord; and he inclined unto me, and heard my cry. He brought me up also out of an horrible pit, out of the miry clay, and set my feet upon a rock, and established my goings. And he hath put a new song in my mouth, even praise unto our God: many shall see it, and fear, and shall trust in the Lord (Psalm 40:1-3).

To my cousin, Debbie, who has always been another sister to me. Watch for her continuous "small role" in this book and, if you read between the lines, you will see the "large role" that she plays in my life. God bless you, Debbie!

Preface

This book is based on the actual murder trial of Richard Jason Veitch, which ended on April 16 2009. With utmost respect for the life that was lost, and for all of those who were involved in the nightmare, many of the names have been changed.

Jason is a handsome twenty-eight-year-old successful homebuilder who resides with his beautiful twenty-five-year-old wife, Stephanie, and their seven-year-old son, J.J., in a small town in Georgia. Jason is a Christian whom the Lord called to preach the gospel in December 2007. This account describes Satan's attack on this young family during the early morning hours of June 28, 2008.

This entire book is written from my perspective as Jason's mother. It is based on the actual events that took place before, during and after his high profile murder trial. It will take you through the legal process, the utter helplessness endured by the family and the strong faith that ultimately brought us to a place of victory.

This is a story that God desires to be told. It is a story about truth, the whole truth and everything *but* the truth! And it is a story that could happen to you or someone you love. It is unbelievable and unforgettable by all who witnessed it. We will carry it with us for the rest of our lives.

This book was finished on the fifteenth day of the month, it has fifteen chapters and it has been fifteen months since the incident happened. Jennifer, my daughter-in-law, informed me that the number fifteen means "rest."

Introduction

When the white van went slowly by, Jason became very suspicious and afraid. He had been a victim of numerous copper thefts in his recently built homes. He had several homes under construction in this very secluded neighborhood, and during the course of this week he had been robbed multiple times. The Friday night of June 28, 2008 Jason hid in the woods to watch his next house under construction, which had not yet been robbed. He had arrived at 10:00 p.m. and now it was approaching 12:45 a.m. He never expected anyone to return, and come Monday he was going to hire a security guard. He was there—just in case.

The van went to the end of the street, turned around slowly, and came back where Jason was waiting. As he sat in the woods his palms began to sweat while he continued watching the van cruise the street. He felt relief when he thought it was gone, but just as he began to breathe normally he could see their brake lights, as they were turning around and coming back. "Oh no, please God, don't let them come here," he thought to himself. With fear mounting he continued watching the van come back slowly, and just as it approached the house Jason's worst fear became reality, as it made an abrupt turn into the driveway, shining its headlights directly on him hiding in the woods.

"Oh God...."

CHAPTER ONE

Earlier That Day

"What a beautiful Friday morning," I thought, as I was closing up my desk getting ready to go to Newnan, Georgia. I called home and asked Mom if everybody was doing well. She said not really, as Jason was robbed of copper again last night. Jason is my youngest son, and has been building houses for the past eight years. In this particular subdivision he had approximately eight houses under construction, and in this one week had been robbed of copper in three of these houses. One night this week he even parked a car that resembles a police car in the driveway of the home under construction, and the robbers went around the car and robbed the house of copper anyway.

"Oh no," I said, "has he called the police?" "Yes," she replied. "They are sending someone from the sheriff's department down to the site this afternoon to meet with Jason and discuss how he should handle these thefts.

Your dad told Jason that he would call Joe Adams this afternoon to see if he has any ideas." Joe is a nice man who attends church with us and he also works for the sheriff's department.

Before I left the office I went to my husband Larry's office and repeated to him what I had been told. Larry is the president and owner of a medical imaging company in South, Georgia. I told him that I was going up to Newnan, and I would speak with Jason to find out what he feels needs to be done to put a stop to the thefts.

As I approached Warm Springs, a beautiful small town that I travel through on my way to Newnan, I thought to myself, "Lord, this is such a nice day. Why did someone have to rob my son's house of copper and dampen the whole day?" Every time one of these houses was robbed it cost Jason approximately $6,000. This was not good considering we were already in a down economy. I decided to call Jason and check on him.

When he answered his cell phone I told him that I was so sorry to hear that he had been robbed again. He sounded very frustrated, and with just cause. Jason had been robbed many times over the past few months of copper in his homes under construction. He had filed numerous police reports, but just could get no relief. The police department told Jason that copper thieves were nearly impossible to catch, because you have to catch them in the act and law enforcement did not have the manpower to do that.

Later on that evening Larry came to Newnan also. We attended a birthday party in Atlanta and afterward drove back to South, Georgia. We were in separate vehicles so Larry left Newnan before me. I went by my parents' house first, and then around 9:45 p.m. I headed south.

At 10:12 p.m. I called Jason's cell phone. He answered, and I asked him what he was doing. He said, "I just arrived here at these houses, and I am going to sit in the woods and watch them all night." I replied, "What?" He said, "It will be fine, I met with Deputy Steven Jones from the sheriff's department this afternoon who advised me that I should watch the houses myself, and if anyone comes to call law enforcement. He also told me that if they tried to leave before law enforcement arrived, I should make a citizen's arrest."

Jason told me that his plan was to watch the houses, and if he saw anything, he would call the police and let them handle it. Jason was told by the deputy that he was legally allowed to have a firearm, he was legally allowed to hold the suspect at gunpoint, and he was also legally allowed to detain the suspect (by binding their hands and feet) until the police arrived.

Jason was told not to shoot anyone and to wait for the police to arrive. The deputy also told Jason the police would be patrolling nearby in case an emergency did arise. Law enforcement would be notified of Jason's intentions to guard these houses on his own tonight.

I told Jason, "I don't like this at all." He said, "It is only for this weekend. On Monday Joe is going to meet with me, and we will figure out something different to do, but he is out of town until then." I told Jason to please be careful, but we never thought the robbers would return again this week. I prayed that the Lord would keep my son safe. The Lord gave me the assurance that He was there also, and Jason was not alone. I then had total peace over the situation.

As Larry and I lay in the bed sound asleep the phone rang. Larry answered it, and I heard him say, "Oh no." I looked at the clock; it was 2:00 a.m. As I took the phone I heard my dad on the other end say, "Jason was down there watching those houses and the robbers came back. He was trying to tie them up, but the gun misfired and shot one of them, so Billy (Jason's father-in-law) is on the way with the wounded man to the hospital!" I asked if Jason was okay and Dad said he was.

I said, "Jason did not tell me Billy was going to be there." My dad said, "Jason called Billy after he called the police." I asked, "Do you think Larry and I should come up there?" Dad answered, "No, just wait until we find out more about it. Your mom and I are going to the hospital ourselves." I hoped the man wasn't wounded too badly and asked my dad to please keep us posted. He said that he would call me the minute he found out anything. I felt Billy would get the wounded man to the hospital and everything would be fine. Next I started praying that everyone and everything would be fine.

After the call from my dad I got up and moved into the living room with the cordless telephone. I stayed in constant contact with my parents and Stephanie (Jason's wife). No one knew anything. No one could find out anything. My parents went to the hospital, but the police had Billy surrounded while interrogating him. Jason was in the back seat of a police car down at the construction site, and law enforcement had confiscated his cell phone. We all felt so helpless, but we felt it would turn out fine. I called my oldest son, Jim, and he entered the loop with us. We were constantly calling each other, yet none of us learned anything throughout the night.

At about 7:00 a.m. I had drifted off to sleep when the phone rang. I felt sure it was either Stephanie or my parents calling to let us know everything was fine and under control. Instead it was Stephanie screaming and crying into the phone. I will never forget the sound of her voice and what she said for the rest of my life: "Jackie, the man died, Jason has been arrested, taken to jail and charged with felony murder. They may arrest my daddy also!"

All that I could say was, "Oh Lord!"

Builder charged in slaying

By SARAH FAY CAMPBELL
sarah@newnan.com

A Newnan builder who decided to take the law into his own hands, and allegedly killed one innocent man and terrorized two others, was bound over to Coweta Superior Court on charges of felony murder Monday.

A probable cause hearing for Jason Veitch, 28, was held before Coweta Chief Magistrate Jim Stripling Monday.

Bond for a murder charge can only be set by a Superior Court judge.

Captain Tony Grant of the Coweta County Sheriff's Office expects "at least three counts of aggravated assault" to be added. There are no charges against Veitch's father-in-law, who witnessed the shooting.

told him 'no,'" Grant said. Veitch then asked if he could shoot them in the leg. Jordan said he couldn't shoot them at all, but suggested surveillance cameras.

CHAPTER TWO

When Can I See Him?

"**W**here is he? When can I see him?" I asked, crying and hardly able to breathe. Ron Harmon, Jason's real estate attorney who handles the closings when he sells a house, was awakened by my dad knocking on his door at 7:00 a.m. Ron came down and met with the family at Jason and Stephanie's home. Ron had gone by the judge's office immediately upon notification of the accident, but the deputy who had met Jason at the site earlier that afternoon to give him advice regarding copper theft had gone to the judge before Ron could get there. The deputy told the judge so many untruths (that would not be proven in court until ten months later), that for now it was being interpreted as the truth. The deputy told the judge that Jason was in a rage regarding the thefts and his intentions were to kill somebody.

The judge told Ron that he did not know this deputy and that he must be new on the force. However, he also told Ron that because of the deputy's accusation he would have to rule the charge as felony murder. The judge felt Jason should be charged with misdemeanor manslaughter since it was accidental, but because of the deputy's accusation the charge would stand as felony murder. Ron told me that after leaving the judge's office he went by the county jail to see Jason. He said that he was holding up, considering what he had been through. I asked Ron when I could see him and he replied that by 1:00 p.m. Jason could have three visitors.

So at 1:00 p.m. Larry, Stephanie and I were allowed—not individually, but together—to see Jason for a total of fifteen minutes. We could see him twice a week afterward. I didn't know what to expect since I had never been inside the county jail. It was divided into pods, with A pod representing the worst of the worst. I refer to it as "Cell Block A." That is where they had placed my son.

They finally called us back to visit. I was trembling inside and what I saw was burned into my mind for the rest of my life. My son came in wearing a red-and-white-striped jumpsuit. (Red and white symbolized murder). With tears streaming down his face and looking at us through the glass, he said, "I didn't mean to hurt anybody; it was an accident. I wish I had not gone down there."

We could not touch him or comfort him. I prayed, "Lord, even though I am dying on the inside, please help me to remain strong so that I can help my son."

I called him by his nickname of "Bird" and told him that it would be okay and that he just needed to trust in the Lord. I said, "I know the Lord was down at the site with you, because He assured me that He was there when I prayed for you last night! You will get through this but you have to stay strong. We will start the proceedings to get you out on bond." That was about all we had time to say before the loud buzzer sounded and they came to take him away. It also sounded like all of the heavy steel doors were locking down around us. That is something I will always remember because it was so loud.

Jason looked so weak and tired as they were carrying him away. Not only was he carrying the weight of the life that was lost, but also the weight of the possibility that he may never leave this place. He may never go home to his wife and little boy. I just wanted to grab him, hold him, put him in the car and take him home, but I could not. For the first time, I felt totally helpless. I have never been in a situation where I could not see or talk to my two sons anytime I wanted. I could not handle someone else telling me what I could do and what I could not do when it came to my child. My prayer was, "Lord, I can't be in there with him, but You are, and I pray that You will keep him safe, and help us to get him out soon!"

Following that visit everything that could go wrong, went wrong. In order for Jason to call us we had to buy him a PayPal calling card. We only knew that because one of the other visitors told us. No one from the facility told us anything. Later that afternoon we did manage to get him a calling card. We all sat around our houses waiting for the phone to ring. Whenever one of us heard from him, we would immediately call the other ones. That was all we could do.

The next day at 8:00 a.m., I received a call from Stephanie informing me that Jason's picture was on the front page of the Sunday newspaper, with the headline: "BUILDER CHARGED WITH FELONY MURDER." How devastating! How could this be happening? It had to be a nightmare, for surely I would wake up soon and find that Jason was home with his family, and everything was great like the day before yesterday!

I called the jail to see if we could visit Jason again and I was told not until Wednesday at 7:00 p.m. for fifteen minutes. Kicked in the stomach again, I called Stephanie to let her know. She went to church to be with her church family, who was a great support and strength during this time.

Little by little the pieces of this puzzling nightmare were starting to come together. Evidently what had happened was this: Three drywall workers had been down at the houses hanging sheetrock earlier in the day. They had left to get something to eat and returned at midnight to spend the night at the site in their van without advising anyone that they were planning to do so. This was their explanation for returning to the house under construction and it was all of the information that we had at this time.

At about 6:00 p.m. on that Sunday afternoon my phone rang and it was my mother calling to inform me that Darrell, my cousin, had gone down to the construction site to check on the houses for Jason. When Darrell got there he was stunned to find the two drywall workers, their attorney and Deputy Jones. The deputy approached Darrell's vehicle and asked him what he was doing there. Darrell explained that he was family and was checking on the houses for Jason. Deputy Jones tried multiple times to provoke Darrell to get out of his truck and talk to the two drywall workers. Darrell repeatedly refused and the deputy told Darrell that he was waiting for Fox 5 News to get there!

When Fox 5 News gave their report, the two drywall workers accused Jason of executing their cousin. That is what was reported throughout the news media. This was getting worse by the minute. The only hope we had was that within hours it would be Monday and the preliminary hearing was scheduled for 9:00 a.m.

GOD HELP US!

CHAPTER THREE

The Preliminary Hearing

To say our thoughts were scattered was an understatement as we walked through the front doors of the Coweta County Court House. With it being a new building, no one knew where to go. It seemed like after we were told, we were still confused. There were a lot of family and friends who had already gathered there. We were finally put into the jury deliberation room where we were to wait until Jason's preliminary hearing began. The only consolation I had was the fact that when I left the courthouse, Jason would be leaving with us, and J.J. would be so excited to see his daddy after being away from him for three days.

It seemed like hours before they came for us. Ron had requested that Stephanie bring a set of clothes for Jason to wear to court, and he would get the clothes to him. Finally, at around 1:00 p.m., they came for us. Nervously, we all filed in a single line down the hall to the courtroom.

They instructed us as to how we should sit once we entered the courtroom, with the immediate family sitting on the front rows, followed by other family members, and then close friends behind them. We were all to sit on the left side of the courtroom, and later I noticed that the media were rapidly filling up the right side.

As the doors opened and we entered the courtroom I could see Jason sitting down front at a table with Ron. He wasn't wearing the red-and-white-striped jumpsuit, as he was wearing the clothes that Stephanie had brought. He turned around, looked at us, and gave a smile. He looked so worried, confused, humiliated and sad, but was trying to remain strong. It broke my already broken heart into a few more pieces. We were not allowed to talk to him or touch him. A few minutes passed, and the judge entered the courtroom.

Judge Strickland announced that television cameras would not be allowed in the courtroom and he then made some remarks to the various media outlets who were seated in the courtroom before turning it over to the prosecutor (Assistant District Attorney Roy Myers). The first witness the prosecution called was the lead investigator on the case, Detective Tom Graham. Mr. Myers questioned Detective Graham about the night in question. Detective Graham read directly from Deputy Jones' investigative report insisting that Jason wanted to kill somebody. This was the first time, during Detective Graham's testimony, that we actually heard the names of the three drywall workers in the van that night. This was the first time we had heard the name of the deceased. Each time we had asked about the deceased we were told that we could not be given that information. After three inquiries we decided to stop asking.

Ron cross-examined Detective Graham, but the detective never wavered from Deputy Jones' report, and even though we knew the investigative report was not true, we had not had any time to prove otherwise. I do believe that Judge Strickland wanted to lower the felony murder charge, but Assistant District Attorney Myers was playing hardball. Mr. Myers knew this was an accident, but he felt Jason should not have taken the law into his own hands, and he was going to make a public example out of him. It apparently did not matter that law enforcement had advised Jason to make a citizen's arrest. That fact was conveniently left out of Deputy Jones' report. There was no mention of it at all. So much was going wrong that I started to feel nauseous. However, I started seeing things more clearly in my mind.

Deputy Jones had set Jason up to take the fall for himself, because he should never have advised Jason to take the law into his own hands, and because Jason took the deputy's advice, somebody died. This was why

Deputy Jones went to the judge's office during those early morning hours, even before we could get an attorney there, so he could tell the judge that Jason was in a rage and just wanted to kill somebody. It also explains why he had manipulated his investigative report and why he had taken the other two drywall workers back down to the construction site within twenty-four hours after the incident, with their attorney, waiting for Fox 5 News, so they could give their side of the story.

"Jason executed their cousin," that was their story. Why were they not grieving for their cousin and why had they filed a pre-suit civil action within a few hours? There was plenty of time for doing that later. How could they even be thinking such a thing at the time? All of these things had been done before we could get the name of the deceased. The bigger the story became that Jason just wanted to kill somebody and that he had executed someone, the better Deputy Jones looked. It now all made sense!

Back in the courtroom, Judge Strickland had just ruled that the felony murder charge would stand. Jason was officially charged with felony murder and he would not be going home with us that day. As the police officer came over to put handcuffs back on Jason, I could see that his feet were shackled. I did not notice that when he was sitting down. He had a hard time walking out of the courtroom and I soon realized that was why.

When I got up to walk out of the courtroom I was in a trance. I could have walked into a brick wall without seeing it. Stephanie fainted in the hall and I never noticed. Family members were weeping and groups had gathered collecting their thoughts. No one expected this, as we all thought Jason would be going home that day. The next thing I knew I was sitting on a bench in front of the courthouse. The television cameras were there and Ron was being interviewed. Larry drove up in front of the courthouse and I got into the car totally speechless!

Friday was the Fourth of July and we always have a barbeque on the holiday. Larry went ahead and barbequed and the family came as always. Everyone tried to talk about other things but all I could do was listen for my cell phone to ring. At 1:00 p.m., as everyone was eating, that call did come. It was Jason calling to talk to everyone for a few minutes. I talked with him for a few minutes, told him how much we missed him, called Stephanie to the phone and then went and cried.

Later that night after everyone was gone, Jim called me and said, "Mama, I know that the police confiscated Jason's cell phone but I just called it and left him a message. I told him that today we had all of his favorite dishes but because I knew what he was eating in jail I was not able to eat one bite." Afterward, I went and cried again!

CHAPTER FOUR

Nine Days in Hell

After we left the courthouse from the preliminary hearing, Jason was transported back to the county jail. Monday night all I could do was cry and it was the same way the next day. Tuesday evening I spoke with my Sunday school teacher, Mrs. Stewart, on the telephone. She said that her husband wanted to have prayer with me. I spoke with Dr. Stewart for a few minutes, and in those few minutes he gave me the best advise that I could have received during this time. He said, "Jackie, I want to give you some Bible verses to hold on to and claim during this time." They were Proverbs 21:1, Isaiah 54:17, Psalms 57:1 and Psalm 37.

Dr. Stewart had just witnessed a miracle in his own life ten months before. Mrs. Stewart was on her deathbed, dying without any hope, and had made it back to a full recovery. Dr. Stewart advised me to move into, and live in, the Book of Psalms, and I did just that.

The following day I was at the CVS pharmacy when I noticed a paperback book on the stand: *Psalm 91: God's Shield of Protection.* I thought how ironic that was since I had just had this conversation with Dr. Stewart the night before.

I bought the book, took it home and started reading. The more I read, and the more I moved my life into the Book of Psalms, the more I began to live in a different way. The strength that I survived on was not my own. Jackie died that Monday night after the preliminary hearing. The resurrected Jackie was now living "under the shadow of the wings of the almighty."

My good friend Cynthia prayed with me often. What a tower of strength she was for me. She started a prayer line from Georgia to New York. So many people were praying, I now know that number was in the thousands. The only peace that I obtained was when I got into my prayer closet, closed myself off from the world, and crawled into the Book of Psalms. I would never have come out of my prayer closet if not for necessity.

Wednesday evening Stephanie and I were able to get back to see Jason for our second visit. I went in with a different attitude. I spoke briefly with Stephanie and explained to her the need of going in there with a positive attitude. She was right on board with me. She was such a strong, brave, beautiful young woman. God has richly blessed me with two beautiful daughters-in-laws. When we went to see Jason we had no tears to offer him but only smiles and encouragement. We had actually made Jason smile for the first time. I told Jason about my new life in Psalms and I suggested that he do the same thing. Ron had taken Jason a Bible when he first went to visit him at the jail. I felt very strong after I walked out fifteen minutes later. In the car it hit me and I thought, "What did I just do? How did I go in there and not break down? That wasn't just me in there, for it was the Lord in me!"

Satan did not like what he was witnessing. The next day at mid-afternoon I received a call from the jail. It was Jason crying into the phone, telling me he could not stay in that place another day and he had to get out. I could hear prisoners cussing and fighting in the background. I tried to stay strong but Jason was having an anxiety attack. I said, "Let me go and I will call Ron!"

I called Ron, explaining what was happening, and he told me, "Jackie, calm down, there is nothing you can do!" How many times was I going to be told this? "Ron," I said, "you have to do something, please!" Then I heard him say, "I will call the jail and have them make sure that Jason is okay."

Later that evening Jason called back and things had calmed down. I don't know where my following remarks came from, so that means they must have come from the Lord. I said, "Jason, I want you to do something. I want you to get a piece of paper and a pencil and I want you to draw the jail cell. Everything that you can see, I want you to draw it. Then I want you to write down everything that you need and you don't have." He said he would do this and we hung up.

I learned the following day that while Jason was in his cell reading his Bible that night one of the prisoners came by and asked him about the Lord. Jason witnessed to him and showed him through God's Word how he could come to know the Lord. Within the next two days there were two other prisoners asking Jason the same thing. Jason started a prayer meeting inside the jail cell. Jason was incarcerated for nine days and then it was time for our next appearance in court for the bond hearing.

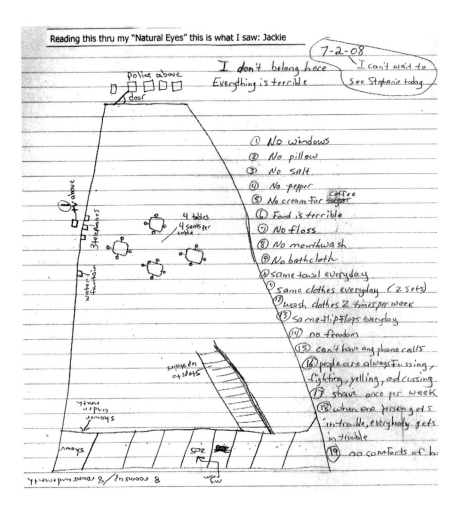

CHAPTER FIVE

The Bond Hearing

The only thing that I knew about a bond hearing was what I had seen on television. It seemed like such a simple process, but like everything else it was anything but. The day after the preliminary hearing Ron and I had a long talk. Ron advised me that he felt it necessary to bring in a criminal defense attorney. It was more than obvious to both of us that the district attorney was going to prosecute Jason for felony murder, even though he knew it was an accident. Ron suggested bringing in Michael Kane as Jason's defense attorney, but Ron also wanted to remain on the case, more as a friend than an attorney, since he cared so much for Jason. Mr. Kane accepted the case and had scheduled this bond hearing. He had advised us to be at the courthouse at 9:00 a.m. in Judge Williams' courtroom.

We arrived at 9:00 a.m. and the courtroom was packed. Evidently, Judge Williams was trying many cases and he was working Jason's case into his busy schedule. This was the Monday following the Fourth of July holiday and you could not have gotten another person in that courtroom. Ron was in the courtroom with us but Mr. Kane was in the next courtroom with Judge Kent, who was trying other cases. We sat there until 12:00 noon, when Judge Williams adjourned court for lunch.

Ron approached Judge Williams and asked him if he would be able to preside over the bond hearing for Jason and Judge Williams advised Ron that he had too many other cases and we would need to come back the next day. Again, we felt as though we had been kicked in the stomach. One more day for Jason to spend in jail was like an eternity to our family. This could not be happening. We had been waiting nine days and nights for this moment to finally get to take Jason home, and this judge was telling us he did not have time to hear Jason's bond hearing even though it would only take five to ten minutes. Instead we would have to wait until tomorrow.

As we left the courtroom none of us could utter a word. Extremely disappointed, we gathered at the elevator. Mr. Kane came out of his courtroom to go to lunch and saw us waiting for the elevator, thinking we were going to lunch. He asked how everything was going in Judge Williams' courtroom and Ron explained to him that Judge Williams had said he did not have time for Jason's case today and to come back tomorrow. Mr. Kane went into Judge

Williams' courtroom, said something to Judge Williams, and returned to tell us to enter Judge Kent's courtroom, which had emptied out for lunch. We were the only family there, along with Ron, Mr. Kane, the prosecutor and Judge Kent. No media!

They brought Jason in from jail wearing the same red-and-white-striped jumpsuit. Seeing him with his hands and feet shackled, I did not know how much more of this I was physically going to be able to endure. Without the strength of the Lord, this vision of Jason would have taken me to the grave. The judge called the bond hearing to order and set Jason's bond at $100,000. Jason was escorted out of the courtroom and taken back to his jail cell. We frantically got out of there and immediately started the process for posting bond. It was already 1:00 in the afternoon and everything had to be finalized by 5:00 p.m. in order to get him out that day.

At 4:45 p.m. we were finally able to pull things together. I picked up J.J. so he would be there when Jason was released, as he had not seen his dad in nine days. We waited for almost an hour for Jason to come out. My mom, dad, Stephanie, J.J., Larry and myself were there waiting. Jim (Jason's brother) and his family, and Jason's cousin Katie were waiting to meet us later.

When Jason came through the door I will never forget the way J.J. shot out from under us and went running into his daddy's arms. What a surge of relief just to finally be able to hug Jason and actually sit down and talk with him. It was the best feeling in the whole world. Even though this case was now just beginning all we cared about was this moment in time when everything was good again.

We took Jason out to dinner at his favorite restaurant. The whole family gathered together and celebrated the victory of having Jason with us. Jason had lost fifteen pounds during his incarceration and he ate like it would be his last meal. J.J. was on one side of him and Stephanie was on the other side. After dinner they left the restaurant for a nice quiet evening at home. It was a bittersweet moment as they drove away from the restaurant. It was good in the sense that Jason would be home with his family tonight, but bad in the sense that the weight of the world was on each of their shoulders. I had to get back home to my prayer closet because I needed God badly at that point!

I will both lay me down in peace, and sleep: for thou, Lord,
only makest me dwell in safety
(Psalm 4:8).

The next morning I woke up feeling better than I had felt in a while. I had a cup of coffee, and just thought back over all of the events of the day before. Especially the part when J.J. went running to his dad. Could life possibly be getting back on track?   As I picked up the newspaper there it was on the front page: Jason's picture along with a lengthy article regarding the bond hearing. There was no way to escape this nightmare it seemed, as the media reports were right there to remind us! The sad part is the fact that what they were printing was not the truth, the blogs were horrifying and we were not allowed to open our mouths to tell the media anything. Anything that we might say could be twisted and come back to hurt Jason's case. So all that was printed were negatives regarding Jason, portraying him as a murderer.

For there is no faithfulness in their mouth; their inward part is very wickedness; their throat is an open sepulcre; they flatter with their tongue (Psalm 5:9).

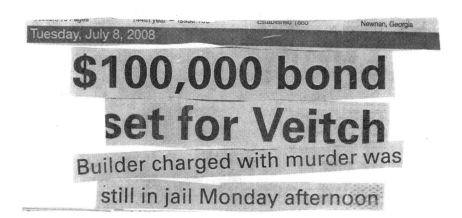

Tuesday, July 8, 2008   Newnan, Georgia

$100,000 bond set for Veitch

Builder charged with murder was still in jail Monday afternoon

CHAPTER SIX

The Arraignment

Mr. Kane told Jason that he was very surprised the district attorney was taking the case before the grand jury in January, as he thought it would be March before it was presented. He told Jason to come to the arraignment alone and to dress down so that he would not stand out in the crowd. Ron had asked Jason to come by and pick him up, so that he could respond to any media questions following the hearing.

The arraignment is the time when the district attorney addresses the grand jury and presents to them the charges for which the accused (in this case, Jason) should stand trial. Up to now we only thought that Jason was being charged with felony murder.

As the judge came into the courtroom it was another one of those "I cannot believe this is happening moments." Many cases were called before Jason's case and that just kept Jason all the more on edge. Finally, case number "2009-SU-R-50 Richard Jason Veitch" was called before the judge.

The district attorney, Roy Myers, approached the judge, faced the grand jury, and said: "I am making a motion to indict Richard Jason Veitch on the following charges: one count of felony murder, three counts of aggravated assault and one count of possession of a firearm during commission of a felony."

The life went out of Jason as he heard each of these additional charges added to the felony murder charge. The grand jury granted the district attorney's petition, and the judge asked Jason how he pleaded. Jason responded, "Not Guilty, Your Honor." "Very well," replied the judge, "the case will be scheduled to go to trial on April 13, 2009."

The judge once again approached the district attorney after the grand jury session and requested that he reduce the charge from felony murder. This case was not a legitimate felony murder case but the district attorney insisted on keeping the felony murder charge against Jason, along with the additional four other charges. Three pleas by judges at different times had been made to this district attorney to lower the charge but he refused to do so.

Jason went to court that morning preparing to plead "not guilty" to one count of felony murder and now he was pleading "not guilty" to five counts. When would this all end? How would this all end? Why does everything continue to get worse instead of better?

"Be merciful unto me, O God, be merciful unto me: for my soul trusteth in thee: yea, in the shadow of thy wings will I make my refuge, until these calamities be overpast" (Psalm 57:1).

Ron and Mr. Kane could not believe that the district attorney was ignoring the judge's request to reduce the felony murder to a lower charge, but regardless of that, Jason was going to stand trial for all five charges.

Mr. Kane asked that Jason and Stephanie, Ron, Larry and myself come by his office for a meeting. How in the world could this be happening? For the last seven months since the bond hearing, with the Lord's strength we had been able to carry on with everyday life. Even with all the weight on our shoulders we knew that Jason was home with his family, and we could see him when we wanted. Now another date had been placed over his head.

April 13, 2009 was only three months away. Do we only have Jason for three more months? How in the world are we supposed to deal with this? There was no way to deal with it outside of my prayer closet. I began to spend more and more time reading Psalms and copying my family weekly on Psalm 91 trying to keep everyone on a positive note. The Lord only knows how hard that had become. The only peace that I had came from God's Word, but that was all I needed.

No matter how discouraged I got, God reminded me that He was bigger than the situation. Once God reminded me of the following: "I created the whole world in six days, and on the seventh day I was finished so I just rested. So do you think this problem with Jason is so enormous that I can't straighten it out?" It became so real to me that no matter what man did God could do more! I realized that I needed to have faith in the unseen and not the seen.

This was the new direction in which I was moving. If I decided to put my faith in the seen, it was all DOOM! But Psalm 8:4-5 painted a different picture for me: "When I consider thy heavens, the work of thy fingers, the moon and the stars, which thou hast ordained; What is man, that thou art mindful of him? and the son of man, that thou visitest him?"

At the appointed time we went to the meeting that was scheduled in Mr. Kane's office. The mood of the day was dreary. It really was not any different from any of the other meetings. We always felt as though we had been kicked in the stomach each time we left a meeting so why should this one be any different? It turned out to be different because a trial date was set. Emily Gray, Mr. Kane's associate, was also in the meeting. She understood how I felt as a mother since she was a mom herself. The problem was how do you tell someone in an understanding way that with all of the trumped-up charges and the new additional charges that the option of a plea bargain was out of the question and it would definitely be going to trial? As sympathetic as Emily was, the words hurt just the same.

Somewhere deep down in my heart there had always been a small hope that the attorneys would be able to come to some kind of terms and offer Jason a plea bargain but now I was being told that the small hope that I was hanging on to was gone! My praying friend Cynthia reminded me later of song lyrics that state, "my hope is built on nothing less that Jesus' blood and righteousness. On Christ the solid rock I stand, all other ground is sinking sand! Our family was mired in quick sand and the only thing left to hold on to was Jesus' hand! This was the first time that I cried in a meeting!

I am weary with my groaning; all the night make I my bed to swim: I water my couch with my tears (Psalm 6:6).

The next morning the headlines read: "Builder Richard Jason Veitch Charged in Grand Jury Session on Wednesday with the Following Charges: Felony Murder,

3 counts of Aggravated Assault, and Possession of a Firearm. Trial Scheduled for April 13th, 2009."

So I cried some more!

CHAPTER SEVEN

Losing Emotional Control

The following week I think we were all in a very somber state of mind. It was like being inside a boat on the darkest night, hardly being able to see the water, and trying to find the right direction. The family had become tense with each other. We had no answers for each other and encouragement was hard to find. We all hoped and prayed that Jason would never be faced with a murder trial, that the attorney would call us any day now to say a plea bargain had been offered, and that call did come through on March 18, 2009 from Mr. Kane.

Mr. Kane called and informed Jason that District Attorney Roy Myers called Judge Williams and offered to drop the felony murder charge to voluntary manslaughter carrying a three to five year sentence. Mr. Kane also told Jason that the judge had agreed to a bench trial instead of a jury trial. This meant the judge would try the case and make the final verdict. Nothing about this plea-bargain was the least bit appealing, with the exception of the bench trial. I had always hoped for the bench trial. I read in one of the brochures in the law office that in some cases the judge would offer to try the case. I felt this would also keep the media circus out of it.

We learned later that the sheriff did not want the case to go to a jury trial because of the way Deputy Jones had handled Jason's situation by giving him bad advice and returning to the alleged crime scene the following day with the two sheetrock workers, their attorney and Fox 5 News. Deputy Jones evidently had no authority to do that and it gave the sheriff's department a black eye. We consequently learned that Deputy Jones' employment with the sheriff's department had been terminated.

Deputy Jones was the primary reason that Jason was charged with felony murder. His false accusations were the underlying factor in the district attorney's case. So when I heard the news regarding the deputy's termination from the sheriff's department, I started to feel just a small ray of hope that the charges against Jason would be dropped. But that never happened.

Basically, what Mr. Kane was saying to Jason was this: "The D.A. and judge have agreed to reduce the felony murder charge to voluntary manslaughter and you will serve three to five years, or if you do not accept this plea bargain, the judge has agreed to a bench trial. He will try the case, he will find you guilty of nothing less than involuntary manslaughter, and you will get one to three years. Either way you go to jail most probably for three years!" Jason was given this information over the telephone.

I totally lost control of my emotions. If ever I had a total meltdown it was that day! I called Mr. Kane and asked him if Jason had understood him correctly and he said yes. He advised me that he wanted to meet with the family on Saturday to discuss all of this. I hung up the telephone and with my hands shaking I started writing Mr. Kane a long letter.

Basically, it said the following: "Please tell me why Jason's case only becomes weaker every time it strengthens itself. The termination of Deputy Jones was a great blow to the district attorney. Why did this not help our case at all? Mr. Kane, do you want Jason to go to jail? Let me give you a few reasons why Jason should not go to jail:

1. He has a seven-year-old boy who needs his daddy.
2. He has a wife who is totally dependent on him as a husband, father and provider.
3. He has a clean record with no prior arrest.
4. He is a business owner who is indebted at the present time for millions of dollars.

5. He has a grandfather who is in business with him, and he too is indebted to the bank.
6. He is certainly no threat to society.
7. HE IS INNOCENT!

What is going on here? We can discuss this further on Saturday at our meeting."

Saturday came and we were all gathered around the conference table in Mr. Kane's office. Before the meeting began I looked at Mr. Kane and asked: "Can you please tell me one positive regarding this case?" He looked straight into my eyes and said: "Jackie, the only thing that you want me to say to you is that this will all be over soon, Jason will be exonerated from all of the charges, and he will be totally free to go back home to his family; but, I cannot tell you that!"

Larry and I were both very upset with the options that Jason was being given. We both had felt positive about a bench trial until we were told during the course of the meeting that Mr. Kane and Emily both felt the judge would give Jason one to three years sentencing. They also felt it would be at the Coweta County Prison Camp and that this would make it easier on Jason and the family as far as visitation was concerned. Ron agreed with the other attorneys that this was the course Jason should pursue.

I could offer no advice, as I only had more and more serious questions. Larry felt Jason should do what the attorneys were advising him to do. I guess at this point it dawned on me that the one ray of hope in being offered a bench trial was not a ray of hope at all. It was just a way to speed things up, save the taxpayers the expense of a jury trial, and reduce Jason's chances of going to jail for thirty years to somewhere between one and five years. What about the fact that he was innocent? Did that not account for anything?

For the first time in all of the meetings Jason broke down. He said, "What you are all telling me is that I should take the least amount of prison time in order to bypass going to a jury trial? However, if I do go to a jury trial there is a chance that I will be exonerated of all of the false charges?" Jason also said, "When we finish with the trial, whether it be a bench trial or a jury trial, Mr. Kane, you will go home to your wife and family. Ron, you will go home to your wife, and Larry, you will go home to Mom. I feel this is something that Steph and I have to think about and discuss further at home."

Mr. Kane advised Jason that the judge wanted an answer as soon as possible as to whether or not he was going to take the bench trial. Mr. Kane also advised Jason that if he did decide to go to a jury trial, there was a fifty-fifty chance that he would go to prison for thirty years.

The judge had advised Mr. Kane that if Jason refused the bench trial, went to a jury trial and the jurors found him guilty of anything, even a misdemeanor, he would give Jason the maximum penalty of whatever charge he was found guilty of!

For the first time in all of the meetings Larry lost control of his emotions. He told Jason that he needed to listen to the attorneys and take their advice. They knew what was best for him. My stomach was in my throat. Before we went to the meeting that morning I went through all of my Bibles and cut out Psalm 91 and each of us carried it in the palm of our hands into the meeting. At that point in the meeting I was squeezing my Psalm 91! It was all I had to hold on to. I realized that there was absolutely nothing more that any of us could do! All we had was God's promises that we were holding in our hand.

Deep down inside of my soul I knew that was all I needed. God is so much bigger than man and so much bigger than the whole situation we were experiencing. When my head was exploding, my stomach was in my throat, and my heart was beating out of my chest, that Psalm 91 in the palm of my hand was the only strength that kept me breathing as I got up out of my seat and got into my car, trying to find the words to say when I had to call my parents and Jim, Jason's brother, who were all just waiting and needing to hear a word of encouragement after the meeting. They also had the Psalm 91 passage in their hands and were praying at home while we were meeting.

> *Thou shalt not be afraid for the terror by night;*
> *nor for the arrow that flieth by day.*
> (Psalm 91:5).

The following day was Sunday. After church Jason called me and said that he and Stephanie had prayed at church about the bench trial versus jury trial. Neither of them could get any peace about the bench trial but they both had peace about the jury trial. They both felt if Jason went before the judge, he would be tried strictly by the book, circumstances would not be taken into consideration, the penalty would be passed down, the next case would be called forward, and Jason would go to jail.

Jason was going to go by Mr. Kane's office the next day and let him know that he was going to a jury trial on April 13, 2009! Larry said, "I have done all that I know to do for Jason, this is his decision!" I felt a certain peace knowing that God had given Jason and Stephanie peace regarding the jury trial. I wanted Jason to follow what God was laying on his heart because that is all we had to go with. But God was all we needed!

The following Sunday I went to the afternoon service at Bible Truth Baptist Church in Griffin, Georgia, where my son Jim is the pastor. I always get encouragement and a sense of "everything is going to be fine" whenever I attend Jim's services. It is a small church family and the people are so genuinely caring. During those ten months so many prayers went up from that little altar, but that particular Sunday afternoon Jim was preaching in the Book of Psalms. I lost track of what he was saying because Psalms was taking me in another direction.

I found myself praying: "Dear Lord in heaven, you are Jason's heavenly Father. As much as I love him, You love him more! Larry has done everything that he can possibly do for Jason and I am in no position to do anything else at this point. All I can do is turn it all over to You, step back from it, and let you take full control, without anymore interference from me. I am mentally and physically drained. Thank You, Jesus!"

It was at that precise moment that I felt a sweet, sweet peace start at the bottom of my feet and work its way up to the top of my head. All worry, doubt, fear and any other emotion that Satan was trying to fill me with, had all vanished. I was at total peace!

Because he hath set his love upon me, therefore will
I deliver him: I will set him on high, because he hath

*known my name. He shall call upon me, and I will
answer him: I will be with him in trouble;
I will deliver him, and honour him* (Psalm 91:14-15).

At about that time Jim was closing the service and I heard him say; "Does anyone have anything they would like to say before we dismiss? So I stood up and testified!

CHAPTER EIGHT

Easter Sunday

As it turned out, Easter Sunday of 2009 was April the 12th, the day before Jason's trial. Easter has always been such a special day to me. After all the suffering that Christ endured, it is such a relief just to know that on the third day he arose to go and be with His Father in heaven. He experienced such peace after all of the torment. And that is what we all ached for: peace after the torment.

The first thing that beautiful Sunday morning my cousin Debbie, who is another sister to me, called to alert me of the headlines in the Sunday newspaper: "Richard Jason Veitch's Murder Trial Begins Tomorrow, Monday, April 13, 2009." Then of course it went into great detail about the whole incident. Unfortunately, the newspaper did not have all the facts since we were not allowed to even talk to them. So what they continued to print had many untruths in it and I knew that many people would read it and form their opinions based on what was being reported in the paper. I also knew that anyone who knew Jason knew it was not true.

After church I had the family and a few close friends over to the house for Sunday lunch. It just seemed no matter how much everyone went out of their way to discuss other things that were happening, everyone's mind was on one thing: Jason's trial the next day. So it was like we were thinking one thing and talking about something entirely different. We just couldn't seem to focus on anything anyone was saying. Everyone's nerves were on edge and it just made for a grim and dismal day camouflaged by the smiles on everyone's faces. Although I guess maybe there was a hidden source of strength in those smiles.

We watched the kids playing and they were so innocent not realizing the seriousness of the situation. All but J.J., as he had a sadness about him. Ever since Jason was incarcerated for those nine days, J.J. seemed to be going into a childhood depression. He tried to laugh and play but it wasn't the same as before. We tried not to discuss the situation around him but at times it was impossible not to since the situation was controlling our lives for the time being.

J.J., along with his three girl cousins (Hannah, Anna Grace and Patience), would always spend the night with me on Friday nights. That had been our practice since they were born. Friday night had always been "Gommi's Night." However, J.J. had stopped spending Friday nights with me. He had not stayed overnight since Jason had come home from being incarcerated. I think J.J. was afraid that if he stayed with me and wasn't at home his daddy might be taken away from him again. Insecurity was beginning to set in on J.J.

I tried so hard to encourage J.J. Each time I heard him pray, whether it was his blessing before eating, or his nighttime prayers, he always ended it by saying, "And Dear Jesus, please don't let my daddy go to jail!" It tore my heart out to hear him pray. It had to be so hard on J.J. going to school, knowing that kids can be so uncaring at times. J.J. attended a Christian school and the teachers and staff were very supportive of Jason. They stood behind him and I am sure that J.J.'s teacher was a strong support system for him as well as a source of strength for Stephanie. She became very involved with the school, from helping the teacher to fixing the high school girls' hair for prom. I think it was an outlet for her. Stephanie needed to stay busy and that was a great way to spend some of her time. I was so proud of her.

I still had the peace in my heart that I had received the Sunday before at Jim's church. I knew everything was going to work out. I wished everyone at the Easter lunch had the same peace. It was more like our very own "Last Supper" before the crucifixion. Would this be the last family meal for the next thirty years? Would this be the last time we all sat down at one time as a family and just enjoyed being together? Things that I had taken for granted for so long now became such a big deal! It sure makes you view everything through a different light. That was the way all of the holidays had been since the incident: the Fourth of July, birthdays, Thanksgiving, Christmas, New Year's and now Easter. I thought to myself, "Thank God tomorrow this will all be over, one way or the other, and this way of life will end. We cannot continue to live in this cloud of uncertainty. The Lord does not want us to live that way." That is what I tried to explain to the family during lunch because God is not the author of confusion!

Jason was going to take the witness stand at trial the next day and testify in defense of his own innocence. Being his mother, I knew he was worried that he might possibly say just one thing wrong and the jury would hold it against him. I knew that he had this fear, even though he never admitted it or discussed it with me. After I read the headlines in the paper on Easter morning, I knelt down by my bed and started praying, "Dear Lord, please give me something in Your Word that will encourage Jason today." I just opened my Bible and began to read the page in front of me. I read a paragraph that said: "I will put my words in thy mouth and I will cover thee under the shadow of my hand." I began to cry and praise God. I couldn't wait to call Jason and tell him. Later on when he came over for lunch, I had torn it out of the Bible and gave it to him!

God doesn't want us to worry or be afraid. As Psalm 23:4 reminds us, "Yea, though I walk through the valley of the shadow of death, I will fear no evil: for thou art with me; thy rod and thy staff they comfort me." God wants us to be sure of His love for us and His promises to us. He wants us to place all of our faith in Him and stop listening to Satan.

I explained to my family that when you stop looking at Satan and keep your eyes focused on God only then will the Lord give you that same peace that He gave me in Jim's church. It is easy to tell someone to do this, but it is an entirely different thing to actually do it. That is why the Lord tells us: "With faith the size of a grain of mustard seed we can move mountains." You cannot obtain that faith the size of a grain of mustard seed as long as you continue to flirt with Satan. You can't think about it or try to analyze it, you just have to trust God and know all will work together for good for those that love Him.

Trust in the Lord with all thine heart: and lean not unto thine own understanding. In all thy ways acknowledge him and he shall direct thy paths (Proverbs 3:5-6).

So much good stuff God has promised us. He gives us all the encouragement that we need in His Word. God does everything that He can possibly do for us but then it is up to us. We decide whether to do what He says or continue listening to Satan. As for me, I have had enough of Satan!

The Times-Herald

CAMPUS

...ps Monday.

Builder's murder trial Monday

Veitch trial Monday

CHAPTER NINE

The Trial: Day One

When the alarm went off Larry and I both were already awake. Without saying very much we both knew this was going to be more than either one of us could possibly imagine. I called Jason and he said that he was fine and they also were getting dressed. The attorneys agreed that J.J. should be there while the potential jurors were being polled. Mr. Kane and Ron both wanted each of the potential jurors to see that Jason was the father of a beautiful little boy. So J.J. was getting ready to go to the courthouse also. We were to be at the Coweta County Courthouse at 9:00 a.m. As hard as all of this was on Larry and myself, I can only imagine what it was like for Jason, Stephanie and J.J. I wondered what they talked about during their drive to the courthouse.

The week before the trial we were given a list of names of the people whom would be in attendance for jury selection and we were also given the names of two judges, one of whom would try Jason. One of the two judges was the one who told the attorney that if Jason took the jury trial he would give him the maximum penalty for anything that he was found guilty of because he did not want the case to go to a jury trial.

I took all of the names and shared them with the family, along with their "Psalm 91" packages. We all started praying and laying hands on each of the names of potential jurors and judges. They were the people whom would meet to decide Jason's fate. But I knew that God was the ultimate Judge whom would decide Jason's fate. (That is where I drew comfort from that day!)

My defense is of God, which saveth the upright in heart.
The Lord hear thee in the day of trouble; the name of
the God of Jacob defend thee (Psalm 7:10; 20:1).

As we approached the Courthouse so many family and friends had already arrived. When we went through security I saw a Christian friend from my past. He was the deputy over the Coweta County Jail. We hugged and I could see the concern in his eyes and the heaviness in his heart. All of us were instructed that the case was assigned to the courtroom on the third floor.

As we opened those heavy double doors and walked into the courtroom I saw Jason sitting down at the front table along with Ron, Mr. Kane and James, a consultant who had been advising Jason on many fronts. None of these three men had advised Jason to take the jury trial but all three were going to give it their all! Behind Jason on the front row sat Stephanie and J.J. Stephanie looked so pretty, but so worried and sad. J.J. had a little car in his hand that he was playing with but I noticed him always looking around trying to figure it all out. He was very nervous.

Jason looked so handsome in his suit and tie. From looking at all of the guys at the front table you would not know which one was on trial. The only way you could tell was by the one who looked the most worried and that was my son. Emily came in and sat with Stephanie and J.J. We were not allowed to sit with her nor were we allowed to speak to Jason or Stephanie in the courtroom.

Mama and Daddy looked worried so my sister, Susie, and her husband, Ronnie, sat on the bench beside them. A few minutes later my other son, Jim, and his wife, Jennifer, entered. That would be the only day that Jennifer would be able to come to the trial. Afterward, she would be picking J.J. up from school and keeping him at her house to play with the three girls until Jason and Stephanie could come by and pick him up after court adjourned.

I noticed on the other side of the courtroom there was another table where the district attorney, Roy Myers, who was prosecuting the case, along with Tom Graham, the lead investigator, were seated. As I looked at the district attorney, he had such a stern look of determination to send Jason to prison. As long as I live, I will never understand why he had such a strong vengeance against Jason. He knew this whole incident was a tragic accident but he continued to prosecute it as something entirely different. How could he do that? How could he look at this young family, knowing this was an accident, and still continue to try to put Jason behind bars?

Behind the prosecutor sat the two plaintiffs, Ernesto Morales and Jose Lerma, along with their family and friends. They all appeared to be very angry with anyone who was there to support Jason. That was the first time that I had seen them, other than when their pictures were in the newspaper and when they were on television saying that Jason had executed their cousin. I also noticed a news reporter sitting in the middle section of the courtroom.

My cousin Debbie, and her mom (Aunt Bet), sat across from Larry and me, and they would look at me from time to time and smile. Debbie's brother Darrell came in later and I was very glad to see him there. A lot of our church family was there also. In time of tests, family is best!

The judge entered the courtroom and we all stood to our feet. We had just received our first miracle, as it was Judge Blackwell and not the judge who had threatened to give Jason the maximum penalty. Praise God!

Judge Blackwell said that the jury selection process would begin. He asked the jurors if any of them knew Jason, or were directly or indirectly involved in the case. Judge Blackwell also asked if any of them had already based an opinion on Jason's innocence or guilt, based on anything they had seen on the television, heard on the radio, read in the newspapers or heard from someone else.

There were forty-four potential jurors and two requested to be dismissed due to Judge Blackwell's questions so we were down to forty-two potential jurors. The selection process went on for about four hours and the jury was selected finally. It was 1:00 p.m. and Judge Blackwell said the court would adjourn for lunch. He instructed everyone in the courtroom that we were not allowed to talk with the jurors or discuss the case in the hallways, bathrooms or anywhere else where a potential juror could overhear our conversations, and after lunch he would hear opening statements.

When Larry and I got into our car to leave for lunch, I immediately called Jason and asked how he was doing. He was trying so hard to be optimistic. He said the attorneys felt good about the jury so that encouraged Jason and he encouraged me. Larry and I ate lunch alone. We discussed all that had transpired earlier in the courtroom and we each had our own opinions about the jurors who had been selected. How could we not? These are the individuals God would use to decide Jason's fate!

When all the worries and fears tried to flood my mind, I reminded myself of the inner peace that God had given me at Jim's church. I claimed it again and I felt God's peace again! These were the jurors and the judge that would try Jason, but God was the final authority and God had already given us the judge we so desperately prayed for.

As we were having lunch and talking I looked down at my watch and it was time to go back! I prayed: "God, so far everything has just been one big mess. It is so hard not to just give up and give in to Satan. But Lord, Jason's whole life is on the line right now. You promised me that you can take the crooked road and make it straight. I am claiming your promise. Please straighten out this mess! Lord, You are the only One who can. Amen."

CHAPTER TEN

Opening Statements

As we re-entered the courtroom, there seemed to be more people present. People that I did not know. Jason was in his place, Stephanie was in her place, but Susie, my sister, had taken J.J. home at lunch, and he would not be back to hear any of the trial. Ron and Mr. Kane had requested that I not bring my Bible to the courtroom. They felt that if any of the jurors saw my Bible it could possibly influence their decision about Jason if they were unbelievers in Christ. I always tried to do exactly as these attorneys instructed me but this was one area where I refused to compromise. I would rather insult one of the jurors than insult God, who was the ultimate Judge and Jury. I had to have my Bible in my hand at all times. I never laid it down in the courtroom. I would turn to Psalms and just read all the encouraging verses and promises that God had given me in His Word.

Then Judge Blackwell entered the courtroom and said that he would hear the opening statements. He began with the prosecutor, Roy Myers, who got out of his seat and carried himself to the podium with self-assurance, presenting an overview of his case to the jury. It sounded so far fetched from what I knew had really happened but I was not allowed to show any sign of expression whatsoever. When I felt like shouting THAT'S NOT TRUE, I would just look down at my Bible and say, "God, You know that's not true."

For, lo, the wicked bend their bow, they make ready their arrow upon the string, that they may privily shoot at the upright in heart (Psalm 11:2).

Now it was time for Mr. Kane to present his opening statement. I was overwhelmingly impressed with what I was hearing. Mr. Kane had really done his homework. He did an absolute perfect job in his presentation. From the very first time that I had met Mr. Kane and Emily, I always tried to get them to see Jason the way that I see Jason. Many times Mr. Kane would tell me, "Jackie, if I see Jason through your eyes, I will never be able to represent him properly. I am here to prove Jason's innocence and that it where I have to focus."

Mr. Kane and Emily had spent so much time getting to know Jason over the past ten months. Ron and Jason had been friends for several years. Ron stayed on the case more as a personal friend to Jason, and a shoulder for us to lean on, rather than as an attorney to Jason. Ron's presence was always comforting to our entire family, and always will be. He stood by Jason and made sure that Jason was represented by the best defense counsel he could possibly have.

When Mr. Kane finished his opening statement I just looked down at my Bible and said, "Thank You, Jesus, for Mr. Kane's flawless opening statement." He stated the truth as to what actually happened down at Trammel Road on Friday, June 28th at 12:45 a.m. I thought of what someone had said to Jason over these past months: "A case built on lies will surely crumble, but a case based on the truth will surely stand!" We had the truth on our side and somehow God would surely untangle this mess but it would take a miracle. There was just too much stacked against Jason with all of these false accusations.

How could Mr. Kane ever convince all of these twelve jurors beyond a shadow of a doubt that Jason was inno-cent of felony murder, three aggravated assault charges and possession of a firearm to commit a felony charge? It was Jason's word against the prosecutor's word and the prosecutor tried to betray Jason as a raging murderer.

That was something that Mr. Kane cautioned Jason about many times during their previous meetings. It is also the reason Mr. Kane, Emily and Ron had advised Jason against a jury trial. However, when Jason and Stephanie got down on their knees and prayed at the church altar about what God would have them do, they only received peace about a jury trial.

I will call upon the Lord, who is worthy to be praised: so shall I be saved from mine enemies (Psalm 18:3).

Satan would try to tell us over and over that with twelve different people, twelve different personalities and twelve different points of view, there was no way Jason would be going home with us at the end of the trial. Satan would bring back images into my mind of Jason in the red-and-white-striped jumpsuit and the handcuffs and shackles. How much can a mama's heart take? Satan knows our weaknesses and if all I had was Satan's lies to listen to I would have given up altogether!

How long shall I take counsel in my soul, having sorrow in my heart daily? How long shall mine enemy be exalted over me? Consider and hear me, O Lord my God: lighten mine eyes, lest I sleep the sleep of death (Psalm 13:3-4).

It was then that God always reminded me: "Jackie, if I created this whole world in six days, and on the seventh day there was nothing else to do so I just rested, why do you think this situation is too crooked for me to make straight? Why do you continue to doubt?"

It was then that I would fall down on my face in our driveway, and with my face to the pavement, I would thank God for the miracle that he was going to perform in Jason's life. As I would get up, look at the dark heavens, and see the stars and the moon, I would know that God is so much bigger than the prosecutor!

CHAPTER ELEVEN

Call Your First Witness

Since lunch we had now heard the opening statements and now the prosecutor, Mr. Myers, was calling his first witness, Deputy Jones. He was the deputy who had met Jason down at the site earlier in the afternoon on June 27th to advise him on how to handle all of the copper thefts that Jason was experiencing. He had advised him "to hire teenagers to hang out in the woods and scare the robbers." He also suggested that Jason "put up deer cameras in order to see who was robbing the houses." He even told Jason that "if he did not catch the robbers himself, they would never be caught."

The main advice that Deputy Jones gave Jason was how to perform a citizen's arrest. He advised Jason to hide in the woods, and if the robbers returned, to call 911. If they tried to leave before help got there, he had the right to restrain them until law enforcement arrived.

He advised Jason that he could hold them at gunpoint, and bind their hands and feet. Deputy Jones had even suggested tying them to a stud inside the house that was under construction since that was the house that had not yet been stripped of copper. And he advised Jason that he would have law enforcement patrolling the area that night since he knew Jason would be down there.

Deputy Jones is the person who was back there at the site within hours after the incident, along with Mr. Morales, Mr. Lerma, and their civil attorney, awaiting Fox 5 News to get there. He was the one who went to the judge within hours after the incident to report that Jason "just wanted to kill somebody." It became apparent to me that the deputy was covering his own tracks because of the bad advice that he had given to Jason. I do not believe for one second that Jason would be on trial for murder if Deputy Jones had reported the truth. He lost his job anyway, so why didn't he just tell the truth upfront?

After the prosecutor had asked his last question, it was Mr. Kane's time to cross-examine Deputy Jones. Wow! This was becoming very interesting. As we knew, during the months since the incident, Deputy Jones had lost his job with the Coweta County sheriff's department. Not only that, but he had lost many other jobs with law enforcement before coming to work in Coweta County. Deputy Jones was full of surprises. The truth about the deputy was finally surfacing and I felt like Mr. Kane had definitely won this round of questioning. We were off to a good start. Thank You, Jesus!

As his next witness, Mr. Myers called the doctor who was the forensic expert with the Georgia crime lab. Mr. Myers and the doctor covered in depth the autopsy report, including a video presentation on a huge screen showing pictures of the deceased. These pictures were very hard to look at but Mr. Myers continued putting them up on the screen over and over. The judge finally told Mr. Myers that it was enough of the pictures since the testimony had moved on to something else yet Mr. Myers wanted to keep the pictures up for the jury to sit and look at.

Finally, Mr. Kane was able to cross-examine the doctor. It was more than obvious that the forensic expert was a witness for the prosecution because he was very reluctant to answer any of Mr. Kane's questions.

As you may recall, Mr. Morales and Mr. Lerma stated that they had been working at the house being built earlier in the day, left around 5:00 p.m., went to eat, and decided to return and camp out at the jobsite later, arriving at approximately 12:45 a.m., without notifying anyone. That is when Jason saw them ride by the site several times and then pull into the driveway, shining their headlights directly upon him. He fell off the bucket that he was sitting on and called 911 to report he was being robbed. He also called Billy, his father-in-law, and told him what was happening. Billy asked Jason if he needed him to come to the site and Jason said yes.

Jason thought for sure that the police would arrive first since they had already been called and were supposed to be patrolling the area. Mr. Morales and Mr. Lerma stated that after arriving at the site, all three of them, including Mr. Carlos', were falling asleep in the van when Billy, Jason's father-in-law, pulled in behind them, got out of his truck and came walking up to their window with a flashlight.

Law enforcement had never arrived, as they were on the other side of town instead of patrolling the area, as Deputy Jones had told Jason they would be. And if that wasn't enough, when law enforcement did respond to the call, they got lost. When Jason saw Billy get out of his truck and approach the van, Jason knew Billy was not armed, as he did not possess guns. This put Billy's life in immediate danger, so Jason could no longer just sit there and watch. He had to take immediate action. That is when Jason came out of the woods, fired a warning shot in the air and joined Billy at the van. Jason was no longer protecting his property; he was protecting his father-in-law.

Mr. Kane asked the doctor several pertinent questions regarding the autopsy report and then he asked the doctor this question: "What did you find when you examined the victim's bladder?" The doctor replied, "The victim's bladder was ninety-nine percent full of urine." Mr. Kane asked the doctor if a person could go to sleep with their bladder that full and Mr. Myers immediately objected to the question but the judge overruled his objection so the doctor had to answer. Mr. Kane asked him again if a person could fall into a state of sleep with their bladder ninety-nine percent full and the doctor answered no.

That totally contradicted Mr. Morales' and Mr. Lerma's statements that they were going to sleep.

Next, Mr. Kane used a wooden doll to illustrate the projections of where Mr. Carlos was shot, and the exact way that Jason had to have been holding the gun in order to reach the projections. The doctor verified that Mr. Kane's projections were exact. Using the projections, Mr. Kane proved that Jason was not holding the shotgun the way you would hold a shotgun to shoot it. He was holding it the way he said, not to shoot it, but to use it to push Mr. Carlos back down, as he was trying to get up.

Jason and Billy had ordered the three men out of the van. Mr. Morales and Mr. Lerma had gotten out with their hands above their head. Mr. Carlos had refused to get out of the van. Jason had no idea how many men were still in the van. He could see shadows moving and it was dark. After several minutes of ordering Mr. Carlos out of the van, Mr. Carlos finally complied. Mr. Morales and Mr. Lerma laid down on the ground with their hands behind their back, but again Mr. Carlos refused. Jason repeatedly told them that the police were on the way and that all he wanted to do was keep them there until the police arrived.

Mr. Carlos got down on his knees but that was it. Jason had no idea if he had a weapon or if there were still others inside of the van. Jason took his foot and pushed Mr. Carlos down on the ground. Afterward, he went back over to where Mr. Morales was lying. As he took out the tie to bind his hands, Mr. Carlos was in the process of getting back up. Billy took his flashlight and tapped him on the shoulder to show him to lie back down but he continued to try to get up. Mr. Morales and Mr. Lerma were also speaking to Mr. Carlos in Spanish, repeatedly telling him to lie down and put his hands behind his back.

Jason thought Mr. Carlos may have a weapon that he was trying to get to or that he was going to try to attack Billy so he went back over to Mr. Carlos. Using all that he had in his hand at the time, the shotgun, Jason jabbed Mr. Carlos in the shoulder to make him lie back down and the gun misfired, shooting Mr. Carlos in the top of his shoulder. It all happened so fast that Jason would have used anything in his hand to make Mr. Carlos lie back down. The gun is all that he had to do it with.

It could not be proven either way in court whether or not the gun misfired. There did not seem to be a problem with the shotgun when investigated by a gun expert but it did have a hair trigger. With the slightest brush against the trigger it would have fired since the top barrel had already fired during the warning shot in the air. I thought to myself, "Why Lord, didn't Mr. Carlos just do like the other two men? Why did he have to be rebellious? He would still be alive today!"

Mr. Kane's projections with the wooden doll proved that Mr. Carlos was getting up when Jason jabbed him with the gun and Jason was not holding the gun as you would to shoot somebody. This removed any doubt that Jason had executed Mr. Carlos, as Mr. Morales and Mr. Lerma had stated in their Fox 5 News interview.

Could it be possible that Mr. Kane had won this round of questioning also? It was about 5:00 p.m. when the forensic expert was dismissed. The judge then adjourned court, stating that court would resume the next morning at 9:00 a.m.

CHAPTER TWELVE

The Trial: Day 2

It was very windy as Larry and I got out of the car and started walking from the parking lot to the courthouse. I felt the day before was a very encouraging day, if there was such a thing in these circumstances. The attorneys felt it was a good day so the rest of the family did also. However, we had no idea what to expect the next day.

As people were filtering into the courtroom, it seemed almost like a different crowd from the day before. Debbie, my cousin, and Aunt Bet sat across from us. My mom, dad, my sister Susie and her husband Ronnie sat in front of them. My son, Jim, was always there, usually sitting either in front, or behind, us. Jim usually brought with him fellow preachers or church family. What an encouragement that was to our family.

On that day my pastor, Jeff Smith, came to the courtroom. Pastor Jeff had always been a strong support system. Cynthia, my praying friend, was a shoulder to lean on also. Cynthia could not be in court with me, but her husband sat on the bench beside me. So precious was he. Mr. and Mrs. Stewart, my Sunday school teacher and her husband, were always giving me encouraging Scriptures to help pull us through. Those Scriptures were my main source of encouragement and hope because the whole court process was totally out of our hands. It all rested in God's hands.

The King's [Judge's] *heart is in the hand of the Lord, as the rivers of water: he turneth it whithersoever he will* (Proverbs 21:1).

When Pastor Jeff came into the courtroom he saw Judge Blackwell and said to me, "I know that judge. He's from Carrollton and he is also a Christian. I taught his secretary's children in my youth group." WOW! That is just what I needed to hear first thing in the morning. I was reminded of how we laid our hands on the pictures of the judges and prayed that God would give Jason this judge, and He did. I had no idea at the time that this judge was a Christian. There is so much power in prayer.

For thou hast maintained my right and my cause;
thou satest in the throne judging right.
(Psalm 9:4).

The judge had the jury enter. I had so many mixed feelings about the jury. I could not read any of their expressions and there was one juror, sitting on the back row, who scared me to death. He was an older man with a stern expression. He looked absolutely emotionless from where I was sitting. All of the jurors, in my opinion, looked as if they could go either way. Nothing was encouraging there!

Mr. Myers called his first witness of the day. It was the first deputy that arrived at the scene. Mr. Myers asked him many questions but he really did not have that much to say regarding Jason because he dealt more with Mr. Morales and Mr. Lerma. He spoke more of his interaction with them. Mr. Kane cross-examined him but his testimony neither helped, nor hurt, Jason in any way.

Mr. Myers called his second witness, which was the second deputy that arrived at the scene. That was the deputy that dealt directly with Jason. Mr. Myers asked many questions but I felt the witness said nothing that could damage Jason. Mr. Kane cross-examined him by asking if Jason was in a rage when he arrived at the scene. Mr. Myers had based his case against Jason on the assumption that Jason was in a rage and "just wanted to kill somebody," as Deputy Jones had reported. This deputy testified that Jason was not in a rage, but was upset that the gun went off. He testified that Jason had already discarded the two weapons that he had on him and had called 911 before and after the incident, requesting an ambulance in the second call.

In a rush for time to save the victim, Jason and Billy had loaded Mr. Carlos in Billy's truck and Billy had rushed Mr. Carlos to the hospital. The deputy testified that "Jason was not in a rage, just upset by everything that had happened." He further noted that Jason was also upset law enforcement had not arrived before the incident took place. He testified that Jason seemed to be more of a calm person who was very upset than a person who was acting in a rage, and it was very apparent that Jason never intended to kill anybody.

I don't know how far this second deputy's testimony went with the jury but it went a long way with me. The deputy stated the facts accurately and I felt a sense of relief from the deputy's testimony.

The Lord is known by the judgment which he executeth:
the wicked is snared in the work of his own hands
(Psalm 9:16).

Mr. Myers called his next witness, Captain Tom Graham, who scared me. Captain Graham was the lead investigator who testified at Jason's preliminary hearing, and we all know how that went. It put Jason sitting where he was sitting! Mr. Myers questioned Captain Graham, who had taken about fifty aerial photos of the site. This was the first time that I had seen where the incident took place. I had not been able to make myself go down to the site. It was hard enough looking at the photos.

You could see the white van, Billy's truck, the two guns, the bucket that Jason was sitting on in the woods, and the place where Mr. Carlos was shot, leaving a circle of blood. Mr. Myers also asked Captain Graham how much ammunition Jason had taken with him. As Captain Graham answered, Mr. Myers sat each shotgun shell up on the rail, counting each of about twenty shells as he set them down. The jury was taking in every shotgun shell also. Later, I asked Jason why he had taken all those shotgun shells. He replied, "Because I had to be prepared for anything, whether it be one robber or ten robbers. I didn't know what to expect so I just emptied the box of shells in my pocket instead of pulling out one or two."

One thing that I did notice from the photos was that Mr. Myers had Jason placed in the wrong area. He had Jason in the woods down behind the house but Jason was in a patch of woods across from the driveway of the house. How could Mr. Myers be off that much? Had he even been down to the site to check out the deputy's report? In my mind, this was a major error.

Finally, Mr. Kane was able to cross-examine Captain Graham. Mr. Kane had picked up on the error by Mr. Myers also. It was one of his first questions to Captain Graham, who had no answer for the question when he realized they had placed Jason in the wrong area. Mr. Kane did an exceptional job with Captain Graham. I felt Mr. Kane got to the truth of the matter and that he won this round of questioning also.

The next witness to take the stand was Mr. Simmons. He was the drywall contractor who had scheduled Mr. Morales, Mr. Lerma and Mr. Carlos, to do the drywall work in Jason's houses. It was a new crew and Jason did not know them. Jason had only met Mr. Simmons one time before. Jason's original drywall contractor was very busy in some of the other houses, so he brought in Mr. Simmons and his crew due to the urgency of getting the houses drywalled before they were robbed of copper.

Mr. Simmons really did no damage either way to Jason. If anything, he was the prosecution's witness, but when Mr. Kane cross-examined him and asked if he knew the men were going to be sleeping on the site and he had failed to notify Jason, he said no. Mr. Simmons was well aware of the copper thefts, and since this was his work crew, it is my opinion he should know if they were going to be sleeping in their van on the property where there had been numerous copper thefts. Mr. Simmons made sure he did not incriminate himself so he simply stated that he did not know they were going to be there. The judge asked the witness to step down and adjourned court until after lunch.

CHAPTER THIRTEEN

Testimony Time

After lunch we drove back to the courthouse, really not knowing who would be the next witness. Nerves were on edge and few words were spoken. Larry and I walked into the courtroom and took our usual seats across from Debbie and Aunt Bet. Debbie's brother, Darrell, had taken off work to be in the courtroom with us. He looked very worried.

Judge Blackwell asked Mr. Myers to proceed with his next witness and Mr. Myers called Mr. Morales, along with his interpreter, to the stand. Mr. Myers questioned Mr. Morales in detail about what he experienced the night of June 27th. Mr. Morales spoke English very well and I kept wondering why he needed an interpreter. Maybe it was to make sure that he fully understood each question being asked of him.

Mr. Morales stated that the three men, (Mr. Lerma, Mr. Carlos and himself), had been working at the house on Trammel Road earlier that day. He said that at about 6:00 p.m. they left the site to go eat, pick up some food for the next day and return to the jobsite to sleep in their van. He testified that they arrived back at the jobsite at about 10:00 p.m. He said they had just arrived at the site and were going to sleep when a truck pulled up behind them and a man with a flashlight walked up beside their van and ordered them to get out.

Mr. Morales added that Jason came up to the van with a gun, also ordering them out of the van. He said that he and Mr. Lerma got out of the van, but that Mr. Carlos did not speak any English and did not understand what to do. He stated that Mr. Carlos got out of the van and he and Mr. Lerma were translating to him in Spanish while Jason was speaking to him in English.

Mr. Morales testified that Jason walked up behind Mr. Carlos and shot him. He then stated that Billy loaded Mr. Carlos in his truck and took him away. Mr. Myers asked him if Mr. Carlos spoke any words after he had been shot and Mr. Morales said, "Yes, 'cousin.'"

Mr. Kane approached Mr. Morales and asked him once again what time they had left the jobsite. This time Mr. Morales answered with a different time. Mr. Kane then asked Mr. Morales where they went to eat and he replied, "At the truck stop." Mr. Kane asked Mr. Morales once again what time they came back to the worksite. Mr. Morales gave yet a different time than before. The interpreter was working extra hard because she knew that Mr. Morales was contradicting himself.

Mr. Kane asked Mr. Morales what Mr. Carlos was doing in the back of the van and he replied, "Sleeping." Mr. Kane asked Mr. Morales if they had a problem finding the site upon their return. Mr. Morales said they rode by it once and then found it. Mr. Kane asked him if Jason helped Billy load Mr. Carlos into Billy's truck after Mr. Carlos had been shot and he said no.

Judge Blackwell asked Mr. Myers to call his next witness and he called Mr. Jose Lerma, along with his interpreter. Mr. Myers questioned Mr. Lerma in great detail. It was apparent from both of the witnesses that they were in this country illegally. When questioned as to how they got to this country, they both had stated they got here by way of the river, and so did the deceased. Mr. Lerma also stated that Jason intentionally shot his cousin. Mr. Myers asked Mr. Lerma if Mr. Carlos had said anything after he had been shot and he said, "Yes, 'cousin.'"

Mr. Kane approached Mr. Lerma and asked him what time the men left the jobsite. He replied that it was about 10:00 p.m. (Mr. Morales had said 6:00 p.m.). Mr. Kane asked Mr. Lerma where they went and Mr. Lerma said, "To eat." Mr. Kane then asked where they ate and Mr. Lerma said, "Arby's, out by Wal-Mart." That totally contradicted Mr. Morales' reply of "the truck stop."

Mr. Kane asked Mr. Lerma where they went next and he replied, "Back to the jobsite to continue working." Mr. Kane then asked him how they were planning to work in the dark and Mr. Lerma replied, "We put up lights inside the house, so we would be able to continue working." Mr. Kane asked Mr. Lerma if they had any problems finding the house upon their return and he said no.

Even though Mr. Lerma was portraying that he could speak very little English, the interpreter was translating every question to him in Spanish. However, I noticed he answered several questions before she translated. Mr. Kane asked Mr. Lerma once again if he was sure they did not have a problem finding the house upon their return and he once again replied no. Mr. Kane played a videotape showing the interview with Mr. Lerma the night he was questioned at the police station. During this interview, Mr. Lerma did not have an interpreter and he spoke very fluent English. In the interview he stated that they did have a problem finding the house and rode by it several times before pulling in to the driveway.

Judge Blackwell asked Mr. Myers to call his next witness and he called Billy Franklin, Jason's father-in-law. Billy was very nervous at first. He and Jason had not been able to see each other for ten months. I can only imagine how he felt. Jason ran to Billy immediately after the gun discharged and hit Mr. Carlos and said, "I did not mean to do that, it was an accident. What do I do now?" and Billy said, "Just tell the truth." Now Billy was testifying about the details of that long night.

Billy answered each question by Mr. Myers to the best of his recollection and then Mr. Kane approached Billy and questioned him. He started by asking if Mr. Carlos was rebellious to their orders and Billy said, "Yes, he was very rebellious. I tapped Mr. Carlos on the shoulder with my flashlight to get him to stay down but he refused. Mr. Morales and Mr. Lerma were telling him what to do in Spanish but Mr. Carlos still refused." Mr. Kane then asked Billy if Jason helped him load Mr. Carlos into his truck after he was shot. Billy said he did and illustrated how he and Jason had carried Mr. Carlos to the truck. (Mr. Morales had testified that Jason did not help Billy).

Mr. Kane asked Billy if he and Jason got blood on themselves when they loaded Mr. Carlos into his truck. Billy answered, "I don't really know, we were just trying to get Mr. Carlos to the hospital because he was bleeding so bad." Mr. Kane then asked, "Did it ever cross you or Jason's mind that Mr. Carlos' blood may have been contaminated, and either you or Jason could have become contaminated by coming in direct contact with Mr. Carlos' blood?" Billy answered, "That thought never crossed our minds. We were just trying to get Mr. Carlos some help."

When the 911 tapes were played you could hear Jason frantically telling Billy to come talk to the operator while he tried to apply pressure to the wound. Jason was urgently trying to help Mr. Carlos and you could hear that on the tape. The previous two witnesses had testified that Jason was very cold and uncaring but the 911 tapes proved otherwise.

Mr. Kane asked Billy if Mr. Carlos had said any words after he had been shot and Billy said, "Oh no, he never uttered a word." The previous two witnesses both testified that Mr. Carlos had said "cousin"! Mr. Kane asked Billy if any lights had been hung inside the house so the drywall workers could continue working in the dark. Billy replied, "No, it was pitch black except for the lights on my truck and my flashlight." Mr. Kane showed pictures taken on the inside of the house that night and there were no lights hung anywhere.

The judge asked Mr. Myers if he had any more witnesses and he answered that the prosecution was resting its case. It was about 5:30 p.m. Tuesday afternoon and Judge Blackwell adjourned court until 9:00 a.m. the next morning. As I walked out of the courtroom Billy was sitting on a bench. I hugged him, told him he did an excellent job and that I was so proud of him. With tears in his eyes, he said, "I just told the truth."

CHAPTER FOURTEEN

Jason's Testimony

Getting out of bed the morning of Jason's testimony was a miracle in itself. I just wanted to bury my head back in the pillow, go back to sleep, and not wake up until the nightmare was over. If Jason was found guilty, I would just as soon not wake up at all. How would I possibly go on with life if that happened? I know that is just being selfish, but that is how I felt as I woke up that morning. How in this world would I continue to live if Jason was thrown into prison with murderers for the next thirty years because of a tragic accident? I would just as soon be dead! That is the point where it became just as much a trial of faith as a trial for murder.

And the Lord shall help them, and deliver them: he shall deliver them from the wicked, and save them, because they trust in him (Psalm 37:40).

I can't imagine how Jason was feeling that morning. Ron and Mr. Kane had both told us that ninety percent of the trial would be based on Jason's testimony. Translated, that means that ninety percent of the mountain was sitting on top of Jason's shoulders. Without the Lord, it would have been more than impossible for our family to survive this ordeal up to that point. But God said, "I will never leave thee nor forsake thee," "I will be with thee in time of trouble" and "All things work together for good for those who love him." I had repeated those verses over and over so many times.

Sitting in the courtroom I was constantly reading in the Book of Psalms. God tells us in Psalms that no matter how big the mountain, with faith the size of a grain of mustard seed, we can move that mountain. God doesn't lie! I had to believe that He would intervene on Jason's behalf that morning in court. My prayer was that God would totally consume Jason's body and speak through him. Jason would not be able to carry that weight by himself.

When we arrived at the courthouse, it was all I could do to get out of the car. Larry was such a stronghold for me. He handled everything so well, even though I knew he was torn apart inside. Larry and Jason are so close. We walked into the courtroom and took our same seat once again. Mama, Daddy, Jim, Susie, Ronnie, Debbie and Aunt Bet, were in their same seats once again looking like they were all ready to burst into tears. What do you say to each other? There are no words!

I had brought a file folder into court with me that morning and I tore out several chapters from Psalms, put the Scriptures into the file folder, and had Ron deliver them to the table where Jason and Mr. Kane were sitting. Ron said, "Jackie, I never thought I would see the day that you would tear pages out of the Bible." To which I replied, "I have other Bibles and Jason needs these verses right now!"

A few minutes before court started I heard something that brought me back to reality: Jason's voice over the speaker system. The 911 tape of that night was being played over the speaker system. The tapes were being checked for audibility before the trial started that morning. I had not heard the 911 tapes prior to that moment. I knew that they existed but I never wanted to hear them.

It was Jason's voice, whispering into the phone, telling the 911 operator to send the police. He sounded so scared and his voice was trembling. As his mother, all that I could think about was, "I should have been there!" I started crying uncontrollably. Larry told me that I had to stop crying before the jury came in or I would be asked to leave the courtroom. With every ounce of my being I forced myself to stop crying. I had to be here for Jason right now because I was not there with him then. Listening to the tapes was gut-wrenching.

The second call to the 911 operator was much more frantic. Mr. Carlos had been shot and Jason was trying to get help. At one point we heard Jason tell Billy to come and talk to the 911 operator while he applied pressure to the gunshot wound. It sounded more than obvious that Jason never meant for that to happen and he was trying in every way to save Mr. Carlos' life.

The prosecution had rested its case so Judge Blackwell asked Mr. Kane to call his first witness, which was Jason. I looked down at my Bible and realized the pages were wet. Then I noticed that my palms were sweating so badly they were ruining my Bible.

Jason looked so handsome in his suit and he looked calmer than I expected. When Mr. Kane asked Jason a question he looked directly at the jury and answered the question. Mr. Kane went over every tiny detail of the case, from start to finish. Jason answered each question with clarity, sounding so calm and assuring as he addressed the jury. After about an hour of questioning, Mr. Kane rested his case. Judge Blackwell then asked Mr. Myers if he would like to cross-examine Jason and he said he did.

When Mr. Myers approached the podium he picked it up and moved it to the other side of the courtroom so that Jason would not be facing the jury. Mr. Myers also stood directly between Jason and Mr. Kane so that Jason could not see his attorney, but Mr. Kane shifted his seat over so that Jason could still see him. I immediately started praying: "Dear God, when I look at Mr. Myers, all I can see is Satan. Mr. Myers knows this was a tragic accident and he continues to portray it as murder. I beg you Jesus, please confound his thoughts and confuse his tongue. Please stop ALL of his false accusations. Please continue to walk with Jason through this valley of the shadow of death. Amen."

Mr. Myers asked Jason question after question, trying every way possible to trip him up. He would ask Jason the same question three times, turning and twisting it around, trying to get a different answer. Jason remained very calm, still in control of his thoughts, and continued to address the jury with each answer. Mr. Myers was getting very frustrated. He became loud, rude and obnoxious, and he started accusing Jason of everything he could think of, but Jason still remained very calm and collected. How could this be, I was asking myself? I kept my hand on the Bible at all times, praying for the Lord to help him!

After about an hour of intense interrogation Mr. Myers said he had no further questions. I could not believe what my eyes had just witnessed. Jason had answered every question in such great detail, with so much clarity, always addressing the jurors, and never did he have to go back and change anything he had said previously.

Mr. Myers had tried everything humanly possible to make him contradict himself in one way or another but it didn't work.

Judge Blackwell adjourned court until after lunch, at which time the attorneys would be giving their closing arguments. Immediately after I got into the car I called Jason's cell phone to let him know how proud I was of him and what an excellent job he did on the witness stand. It was then that he told me that he had the Scripture in his pocket that I had torn out of the Bible on Easter Sunday. The Scripture said, "I will put my words in thy mouth, and I will cover thee under the shadow of my hand." It was then I realized that was not Jason testifying, it was the Lord God speaking directly through his mouth. That is why his testimony was flawless. In Jason's own strength that would have been impossible. I started thanking God over and over that he had carried Jason through the most traumatic time in his life, when I could do nothing at all to help him.

At lunch, as our family talked among ourselves, we all were in agreement that Jason had done an excellent job on the witness stand. After we had eaten we went directly back to the courtroom. The attorneys and the judge were going over some things and I wanted to get with Ron to see how he felt about Jason's testimony. Not only was I able to speak with Ron but Mr. Kane also before court re-adjourned. They both told me how proud they were of Jason and they both felt he could not have done a better job! Their exact words were, "Jason's testimony was flawless."

Judge Blackwell announced that he would hear closing arguments and he began with Mr. Kane. This made me nervous, because I wanted the last thing on the jury's mind before going into deliberations to be Mr. Kane's closing argument. As it stood, they would be hearing Mr. Myers closing argument before going in to deliberations.

Mr. Kane outdid himself with his closing argument. He was the best criminal defense attorney for my son. Mr. Kane presented a timeline slide presentation and using cell phone records he was able to back up all of Jason's testimony. He presented two wooden statues, one portraying the shotgun and the other Mr. Carlos. He presented an illustration board that had two men on it, illustrating the position that Mr. Carlos was in when the gun fired. It plainly showed he was not on the ground, but getting up. It also proved that Jason was not holding the gun as you would if you were going to shoot somebody, but he was holding it the way you would hold any instrument that you would use to push somebody back down with.

Mr. Kane put a slide up on the wall for the jury to see. The slide listed each charge and the meaning of that particular charge. He began with the first charge of felony murder and proved to the jury why Jason was not guilty of felony murder. He went down the line of individual charges, proving to the jury that Jason was not guilty of any of the charges. Mr. Kane then requested that the jury come back with a not guilty verdict on all the charges.

Judge Blackwell then asked Mr. Myers to deliver his closing argument. Mr. Myers gave a thirty-minute presentation to the jury, explaining why he felt Jason should be convicted on all charges. He used the gun, the ammunition and his aerial shots to try to prove his point. At one point he kept demanding over and over that the jury had to come back with a guilty verdict. He told the jury they had no choice but to find Jason guilty.

Judge Blackwell intervened at that point and disciplined him. I kept my hand on the Bible and prayed that the Lord would confound Mr. Myers' thoughts, and confuse his tongue.

For I have heard the slander of many: fear was on every side: while they took counsel together against me, they devised to take away my life. But I trusted in thee, O Lord: I said,
Thou are my God (Psalm 31:13-14).

It was approximately 4:30 p.m. when the closing arguments had concluded. Judge Blackwell charged the jury, covering each of the charges in-depth and spending about thirty to forty-five minutes addressing the jury. Not knowing how long the jury would be deliberating, the judge told them that he would stay there all night or however long they wanted him to be there. If they wanted to go home and resume the next day, all they had to do was come back to him with that request. He then dismissed them for deliberation.

Thank God that part of the trial was over! We all stood up and stretched our legs. We talked softly among ourselves and we were able to speak with Mr. Kane and Ron as well. We could now speak to Jason and Stephanie in the courtroom for the first time. Stephanie had held up well during the process and so had Jason. However, I am sure that behind the facade they both had the same gut-wrenching feeling Larry and I and the rest of the family had.

At about 6:30 p.m. the bailiff came back to the judge with a note from the jury requesting to be adjourned until 9:00 a.m. the next day and the judge granted their request. They had been deliberating for about an hour and still needed more time. We didn't know whether that was good or bad yet those were the questions we each took home with us.

GOD'S SHIELD OF PROTECTION

PSALM 91

We Are Claiming Our Miracle....

CHAPTER FIFTEEN

The Verdict

Thursday, April 16, 2009 would prayerfully be the day that the world of torment would end, one way or the other. If the verdict was guilty, I would rather go back to last month, or the month before that. I would rather live with the uncertainty of not knowing than knowing, if the verdict was guilty. My son's life was on the line that day. I cannot imagine how he and Stephanie were feeling as they woke up and got dressed for court that day. Would it be the last morning they woke up together, got dressed together, had coffee together and got J.J. off to school together? I could not comprehend how hard it must have been for Jason to say goodbye to J.J. as he dropped him off at school that morning. It was all so unbearable!

I called Jason's cell phone on the way to the courthouse. He answered and very briefly tried to sound upbeat but I know him. Jason said they were okay and would see me at the courthouse.

As we walked into the courtroom everything seemed different. Nobody was sitting in the seats they had sat in all week. It was confusion! Everyone was standing in small groups talking. What were they all talking about? Trying to figure out the verdict no doubt! No one said anything to me but they were all talking about it among themselves. I had become immune to small talk many months ago!

Stephanie was sitting on the front row behind Jason, who was at the front table with Ron and Mr. Kane. I went down and sat beside Stephanie. Larry mingled with the different groups. I am glad that Larry could do that because I had no energy left within me to mingle. Ron and Mr. Kane tried to keep us encouraged, but not encouraged, at the same time. Both of them kept reiterating the fact that it had been an absolutely flawless defense, and that would lift us up. I knew that only God could have provided that. However, they would also immediately let us know that no matter what the outcome, everything that could be done, was done. And that would bring us right back down.

I sat over in the corner on the front row and began reading my Bible. That day it was Psalm 31:15-16,18 that lifted my spirits: "My times are in thy hand: deliver me from the hand of mine enemies, and from them that persecute me. Make thy face to shine upon thy servant:

save me for thy mercies' sake. Let the lying lips be put to silence; which speak grievous things proudly and contemptuously against the righteous." It was always the Psalms that made me feel better.

People could not help me in a time like that. People will tell you what you want to hear, just to make you feel better. Everyone except Ron and Mr. Kane, that is. There are those people who don't have a clue what to say to you, and then there are those who just don't say anything. That is why I chose to talk with God. He was the only One who could deliver Jason from that night-mare. He was the only One who had encouraging words on which I could depend.

Many sorrows shall be to the wicked: but he that trusteth in the Lord, mercy shall compass him about (Psalm 32:10).

It was 12:00 noon and the jury was still deliberating so the judge dismissed us for lunch. After lunch, when we returned back to the courthouse, I spoke to the family and friends who had arrived back and requested that we form a circle outside the courtroom and pray for the jury. I found a bench that I converted into an altar. Jim, my oldest son, led the group in prayer. Ron and Mr. Kane had returned back from lunch just as we had begun to pray but they did not interrupt us. They both knew how important prayer was to our family.

It was not until about 3:30 p.m. that we were notified the jury had reached a verdict. I cannot describe what I felt at that point. Mr. Kane was instructing each of us as to where he wanted us to sit in the courtroom. He placed Larry and myself on the front row in the middle section. Stephanie was placed on the front row directly behind Jason. Jim, my mom, dad, sister and brother-in-law were behind Larry and myself, in the middle section. Other family and friends were scattered around us. The media were also stationed behind the middle section, with their television crew and cameras. A reporter from the newspaper was sitting on the front row to the left of me. The courtroom was packed and I do not think you could have fit another person in it.

Judge Blackwell called in the jury. There was a man on the jury that had scared me from the very beginning. He was an older man without any expression and was the hardest person on the jury to read. Even the jurors that we felt we could read were not all positive. However, this one man really frightened me.

As the jury filed back into the jury box, Larry reached over and whispered to me, "I think that man we were concerned about is the foreman of the jury!" "Oh no," I said. "God, please help us!"

The judge asked the jury if they had reached a decision and that same man we were so concerned about, who was the foreman of the jury as we suspected, said that they had. The verdict was delivered to the judge! Larry was squeezing my hand tightly and I felt as though I was about to hyperventilate. Jason, Ron and Mr. Kane were asked to stand up. For the rest of my life, I will never forget the way Jason looked, standing there between his two attorneys, with the remainder of his life dangling over a cliff! Oh how I wish I could have swapped places with him! Stephanie was just looking straight ahead, as in a trance. I prayed that God would help her and give her the strength to accept whatever came next because she had to be strong for J.J.

I am forgotten as a dead man out of mind:
I am like a broken vessel (Psalm 31:12).

The judge looked at the verdict, but before he read it, he gave the following orders to everyone in the courtroom: "One man is deceased, and another man's life is hanging in the balance. There will be absolutely no outburst in my courtroom after the verdict has been read!"

Charge: Verdict:

One Count Felony Murder   NOT GUILTY

Larry put his arm around me and I started crying. Ron had his arm around Jason but we were not done yet.

Charge: Verdict:

Voluntary Manslaughter   NOT GUILTY

Involuntary Manslaughter   NOT GUILTY

Three Counts Aggravated Assault NOT GUILTY

I put my head in my lap and started sobbing loudly so Larry leaned down on top of me.

Charge: Verdict:

One Count Firearm Possession NOT GUILTY

As I stood up, all that I was able to do was put both of my hands in the air and repeat over and over and over, "Thank You, Jesus! Thank You, Jesus! Thank You, Jesus!" I grabbed Larry and continued to cry, "Thank You, Jesus! Thank You, Jesus! As I came to my senses, I saw Jason and Ron hugging each other and weeping. Stephanie had her hands in the air saying, "God is so merciful, God is so good!" God was there and His presence was overpowering us. Praises were going up all over the courtroom. It was as if someone had just gotten saved, and then I realized that is exactly what had just happened. God had just saved Jason for the second time. Everyone was crying and rushing down to hug Jason, Ron and Mr. Kane.

I hardly remember walking over to Jason but I do remember grabbing him, crying and continuing to say, "Thank You, Jesus!" That was all that would come out of my mouth. When I hugged Mr. Kane, all I could do what put my head on his chest and cry. And it was the same when I hugged Ron. Mr. Kane and Ron were crying right along with the rest of our family. It was truly a miracle from God. There is nothing anyone could ever say, now or ever, to prove otherwise.

Jason and Stephanie were escorted out of the courthouse by one of the deputies. As they were approaching their vehicle, Stephanie saw the foreman of the jury going to his vehicle. She cried, "Sir, wait a minute." She started running toward him crying, and he started running toward her crying. She grabbed him, hugged him, and thanked him from the bottom of her heart. He told her "that all of the jurors were in one accord and he could feel God's presence in the deliberation room!" Jason ran to them and all three of them were hugging and crying in the parking lot. That man, whom I was most concerned about, whom I had never seen before, and whose name I didn't even know, turned out to be an angel from God!

For he shall give his angels charge over thee,
to keep thee in all thy ways (Psalm 91:11).

Everyone in that courtroom witnessed a miracle on April 16, 2009 at 3:45 p.m. None of us who were there will ever forget that day for the rest of our lives. I will never forget the pain that we all endured for ten months. I will never forget the details of the trial, and most importantly, I will never forget how God came down into that courtroom and poured us out a great big MIRACLE. God had answered my prayer!

Never, ever underestimate the power of prayer. Without God, I would never have survived that storm in my life. My life will never be the same. I will never miss an opportunity to testify about that miracle. Every time I drive by the courthouse, I raise my hands once again and thank God for sparing Jason's life. It was a miracle that God demanded to be shared with others who may be going through a storm in their own lives.

Even if you are not in the middle of a storm today, it doesn't mean you will not be going through one tomorrow, or next week. On June 27, 2008 our life was good. It was just the usual ups and downs of everyday life, nothing out of the ordinary. But in the matter of a few hours all our lives changed and our entire family was caught up in the middle of the storm. But God rescued us from the storm and He can rescue you also if you will cry out for His salvation!

I waited patiently for the Lord; and he inclined unto me, and heard my cry. He brought me up also out of an horrible pit,
out of the miry clay, and set my feet upon a rock, and established my goings. And he hath put a new song in my mouth, even praise unto our God: many shall see it, and fear, and shall trust in the Lord
(Psalm 40:1-3).

Coweta track championships held at Drake Stadium
— see results on page 6

POLLEN COUNT **286** Extremely high
POLLENS PRESENT: Oak, sweetgum and sycamore
Thursday's count for metro Atlanta

Confederate Memorial Day Saturday
— see page 3

The Times-Herald

1 Section, 12 Pages   145th year — Issue 107   Established 1865   Newnan, Georgia   ISSN. NO 0883-2926   50 cen

Friday, April 17, 2009   Coweta's Local Daily

Veitch cleared of all charges

By ALEX McRAE
alex@newnan.com

A Coweta County Superior Court jury found Newnan builder Jason Veitch not guilty of felony murder and four other charges in the June 28, 2008, shooting death

We have "Claimed Our Miracle"

Matthew 17:20 KJV

20 And Jesus said unto them, Because of your unbelief: for verily I say unto you, If ye have faith as a grain of mustard seed, ye shall say unto this mountain, Remove hence to yonder place; and it shall remove; and nothing shall be impossible unto you.

Jim and Jennifer Veitch
"Brother"

We have "Claimed Our Miracle"

We have "Claimed Our Miracle"

Cousins   Hannah, Anna Grace, Patience
with JJ

Jack and Mary Jo Duncan
"Grandparents"

For with God nothing shall be impossible... Luke 1:37

We have "Claimed Our Miracle"

Larry and Jackie Carpenter
"Parents"

Having survived this most horrific nightmare, and come out of it only by the "Miracle" that God saw fit to grant us, I knew that I could not just sit back and remain silent. My desire is to give someone else the same encouragement, hope, and inspiration that I received. I am giving you "Jesus"!

Step quietly into your "Prayer Closet"; just you and your Bible. Sit down, relax, pour your need out before the Lord, and then read PSALMS 91. He has every answer that you need right there in the Book of Psalms.

Just remember one thing before you do this: Have you ever received God's free "Gift of Salvation"? The best decision that you will ever make is <u>accepting</u> Christ as your "Lord and Savior".

It is so wonderful having God on our side, fighting all those battles that we are too weak to fight!

WHAT AN AWESOME GOD WE SERVE!

God Bless You

Jackie Carpenter
Jackie Carpenter

Breinigsville, PA USA
24 June 2010
240560BV00002B/1/P